Little Red Head

The Great Western Greenway

Dedicated to the Young Explorers of the World

Written by

Gemma Henry McLoughlin

gemmcloughlin15@gmail.com

Illustrated by

Phillip Foley

phillfoleyart@gmail.com

Published by Mammy Red Head Publications, Text & Illustrations Copyright 2019, Gemma Henry McLoughlin, ISBN 9781912612062,

This is Little Red Head, he likes going on adventures around the island of Ireland. Where will he explore today?

ACHILL ISLAND
NEPHIN BEG MOUNTAINS
MULRANNY
NEWPORT
CLEW BAY
CLARE ISLAND
WESTPORT
CROAGH PATRICK
ittle Red Head is going on
he Great Western Greenway
ı County Mayo, a cycle and
ˈalking path that covers a
istance of 42 kilometres. What
ın will Little Red Head have and
ˈho will he meet along the way?

Little Red Head starts his adventure at the 16th century Westport House, where the land and waters of Connacht were once ruled by the Pirate Queen, Grace O'Malley.

Little Red Head, his sister Mini Miss, and his Mammy and Daddy get ready to get on their bikes and begin their adventures on The Great Western Greenway.

The Great Western Greenway sta
in Westport and goes through t
towns of Newport and Mulran
and then on to Achill Island. T
greenway is the longest off-ro
walking and cycling trail in Irelar

In 1894, the Westport railway line was completed, going as far as Achill. Today, The Great Western Greenway is on the old railway line. Little Red Head rings the bell that was once used to let people know the train was on the way.

The Town of Newport is the first stop for Little F
Head. He loves the 19th century red sandstc
viaduct that he sees as he cycles into the town. Li
Red Head is heading to the famous Kelly's Butch
for some of its renowned Kelly's pudding. Little F
Head loves to eat black pudding for his breakf

Little Red Head gets off his bike and he and his sister do some bird spotting. Little Red Head can see a Golden Plover in the distance. This is a rare bird. Then Mini Miss points out the Grey Heron, which can be found all around the North West of Ireland and along The Great Western Greenway.

There are many winding bridges along the greenway. Little Red Head loves the colourful bridges. The railway line that the greenway follows from Westport to Achill was once a busy hauling line and closed in 1937. As Little Red Head cycles along the route he sees lots of reminders of the railway line and the trains.

Little Red Head and Mini Miss are
hoping that as they cycle the greenway
they will spot some of their favourite
animal friends along the way.
Mini Miss would like to see a fox and Little Red
Head would like to see a long-eared owl.

time for lunch and Little Red Head and Mini Miss sit down
l enjoy their picnic which has lots of yummy goodies to eat.
ey enjoy eating wild Atlantic salmon with Carrowholly cheese on
la bread and they sip their water flavoured with wild flowers.

Little Red Head stands on the greenway at Mulranny and looks over at Clew Bay. Little Red Head thinks the islands look like little green leprechaun homes.

It is said that Clew Bay is made up of 365 islands - one for every day of the year.

Little Red Head and Mini Miss love to build sandcastles and look for crabs and sea creatures. There are lots of periwinkles and mussels to pick and Little Red Head will get them cooked up for his dinner.

Standing on the beach in Mulranny, Little Red head looks out at Croagh Patrick Mountain the third highest mountain in Mayo, Little Red Head would like to climb Croagh Patrick one day.

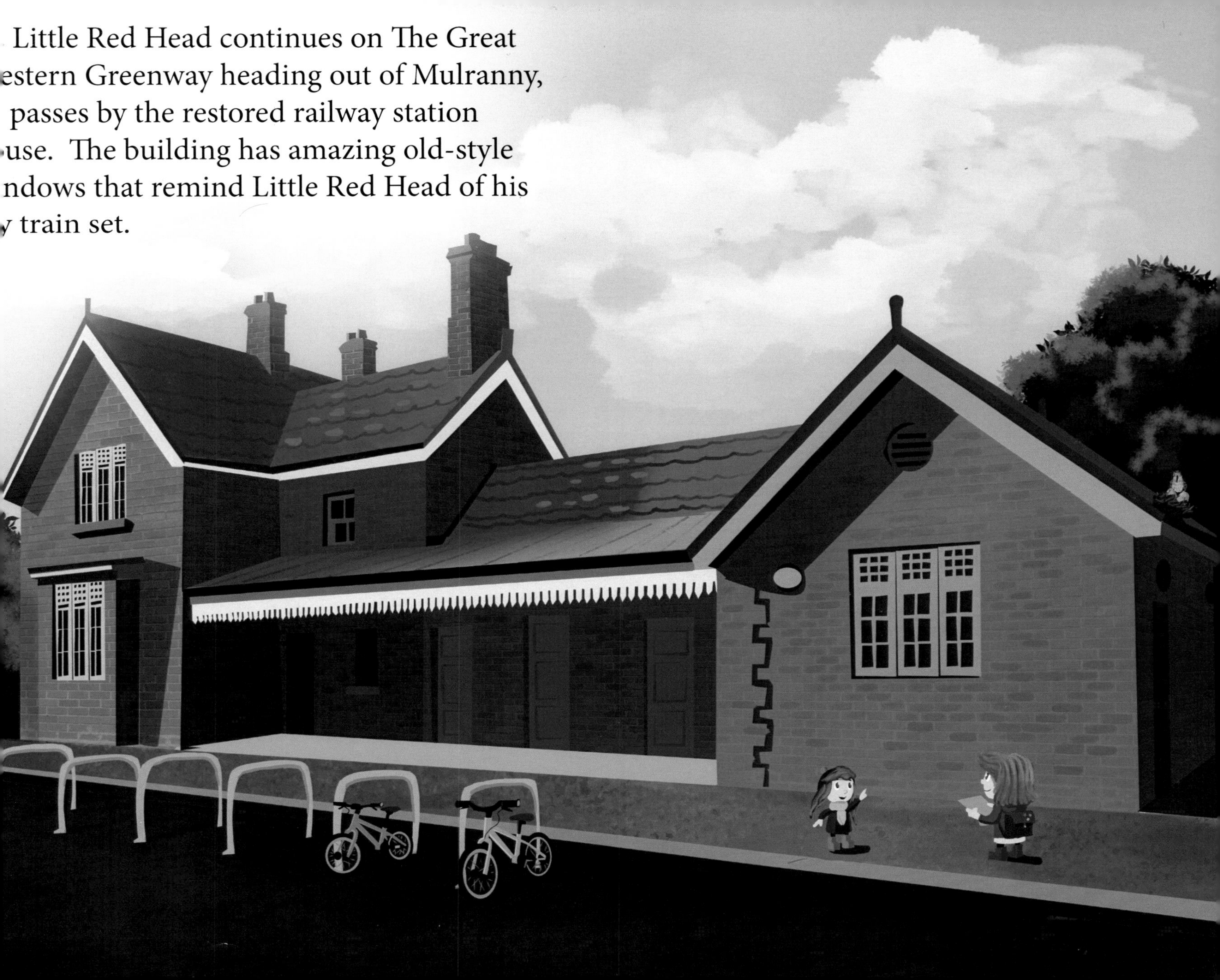

Little Red Head continues on The Great
estern Greenway heading out of Mulranny,
passes by the restored railway station
use. The building has amazing old-style
ndows that remind Little Red Head of his
y train set.

The Great Western Greenway has so many flowers, fauna, grasses and mosses all along the cycle path.

Little Red Head loves the Mediterranean Heather; a purple flower famous because it can only be found growing in Mayo, Ireland, Spain and Portugal.

There is a lot of bog in Ireland and as Little Red Head looks around the greenway, he thinks that Ireland is lucky to have so much rain because it helps the bog, the landscape, the flowers and the animals.

Across the fields in the distance is Wild Nephin Ballycroy National Park, Little Red Head has enjoyed many days of fun there exploring the bog, terrain and all the wildlife.

ıe lakes along The Great Western
reenway make for many adventures
ke fishing and water sports. Little Red
ead and Mini Miss are going to try
ıt kayaking in Achill, they are very
cited.

Little Red Head enters Achill Island by cycling across the Mich
Davitt Bridge. Little Red Head calls it the shark's belly bridge. T
swinging bridge is very big. It is over 6 metres wide and over 2
metres long and it weighs 390 tonnes. Little Red Head starts to ped
fast across the bridge because he can see a boat approaching and t
bridge needs to be manually moved so that the boat can get throug

It's time for Little Red Head to get his toes wet and see can he spot any dolphins or Basking sharks from the sea shore. Little Red Head and Mini Miss are on Keem beach where you can see the massive Croaghaun Mountain, one of the biggest sea cliffs in Europe, measuring 688 metres.

Little Red Head, Mini Miss, Mammy and Daddy have had an amazing time on The Great Western Greenway. Tonight they are going to roast marshmallows and will sleep under the starry night sky. Little Red Head will dream of the amazing sights, tastes and smells he experienced along The Great Western Greenway.

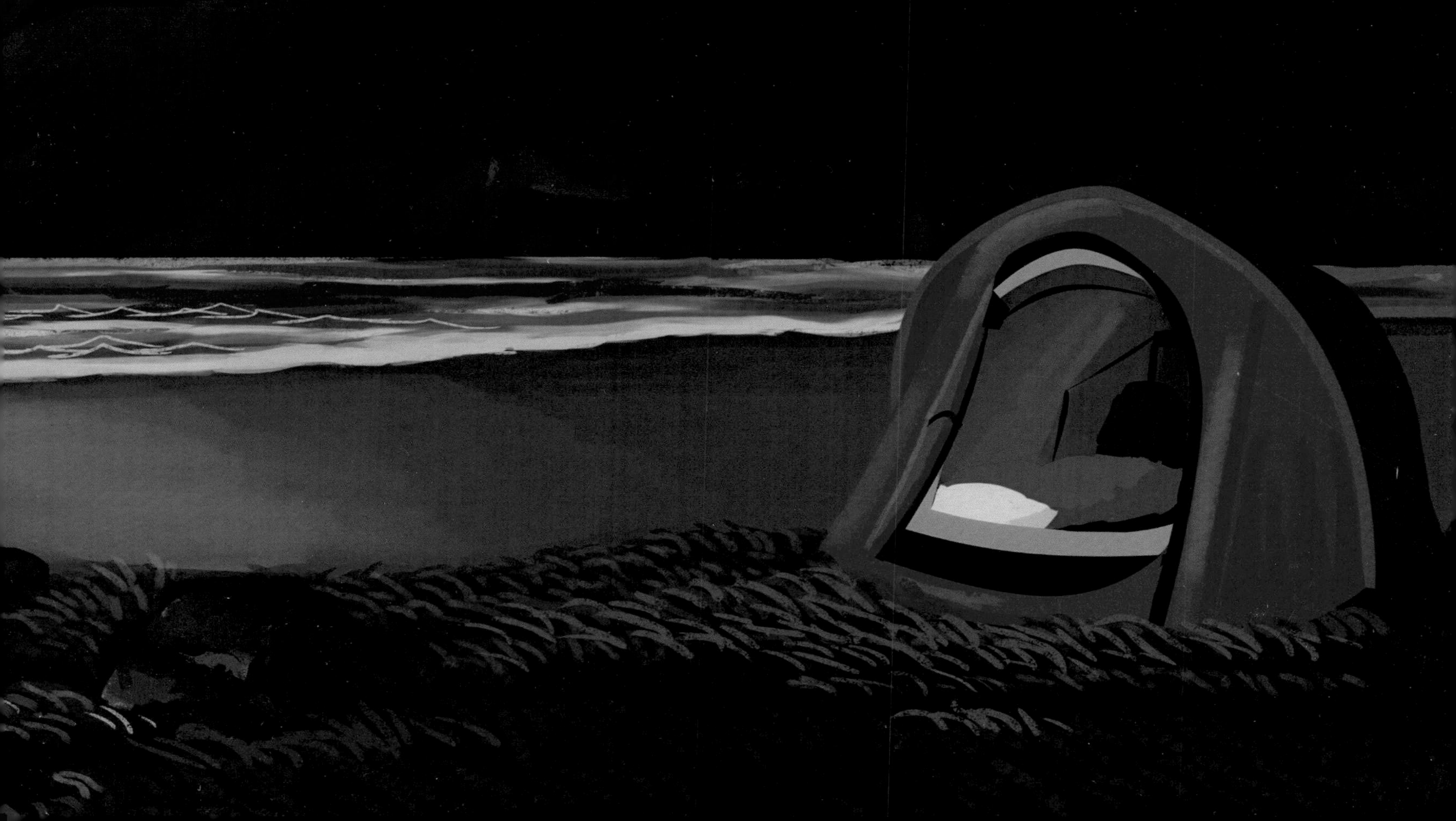

The Great Western Greenway Info

Westport to Newport

- Distance: 11 km
- Terrain: Greenway off road cycle and walking trail
- Estimated Time Cycling: 1 to 1.5 Hours
- Estimated Time Walking: 3 to 3.5 Hours
- Suitable for people with moderate levels of fitness
- Minimum Gear: Helmet, Bike, Mobile Phone, Snacks, Fluid and waterproofs
- Services: Services available Westport and Newport

Newport to Mulranny

- Distance: 18 km
- Terrain: Greenway off road cycle and walking trail
- Estimated Time Cycling: 2 to 2.5 Hours
- Estimated Time Walking: 5 to 5.5 Hours
- Suitable for people with moderate levels of fitness
- Minimum Gear: Helmet, Bike, Mobile Phone, Snacks, Fluid and waterproofs
- Services: Services available Newport and Mulranny

Mulranny to Achill

- Distance: 13 km
- Terrain: Greenway off road cycle and walking trail
- Estimated Time Cycling: 1 to 1.5 Hours
- Estimated Time Walking: 2 to 2.5 Hours
- Suitable for people with moderate levels of fitness
- Minimum Gear: Helmet, Bike, Mobile Phone, Snacks, Fluid and waterproofs
- Services: Services available on Achill Island and Mulranny

Want to find out more about Mammy Red Head ?

Check out; www.mammyredhead.com

Books in the Little Red Head Collection

Céide Fields

Belleek Woods

The Great Western Greenway

look out for more adventures coming soon!